Raining Butterflies

Poetry For Healing The Heart

Poetry, quotes, and other thoughts

This book is mostly about personal experiences in my life - but it's for anyone
that needs some hope and healing

Cherries Chamberlain

Request written permission below:

Cherries Chamberlain
P.O.Box 240836
Apple Valley, MN 55124

cherrieschamberlainwriting@gmail.com

First Edition: August 2024

ISBN: 979-8-218-47136-1   Paperback
Library of Congress Control Number :   2024914470

Publisher's Cataloging- in-Publication data

Names: Chamberlain, Cherries, author.
Title: Raining Butterflies / Cherries Chamberlain.
Description: Apple Valley, MN: Cherries Chamberlain, 2024.
Identifiers: LCCN: 2024914470 | ISBN: 979-8-218-47136-1 (paperback)
Subjects: LCSH Poetry, American - 21st century. | BISAC POETRY /
General | POETRY / Subjects & Themes / Death, Grief, Loss
Classification: LCC PS3603 .H43 R35 2024 | DDC 811.6-dc23

Illustrations and cover designs by Cherries Chamberlain

She believes in

Butterflies

And

Love stories

— Cherries Chamberlain

To my daughters

Always
remember

You have

Wings

Raining Butterflies Book Title Inspiration

I couldn't decide on a title for this book. There was a day last summer that I saw four monarch butterflies within a couple hours of each other in different cities. I couldn't sleep that night as I was thinking about the butterflies and how special it was to see four of them in the same day and then I started thinking about what they represent. Spiritually, butterflies are a symbol of hope, strength, endurance, change, new direction, and transformation. This is all similar to what Ive been feeling in my own life. That I needed to find my wings again. This book title comes from all the love, loss, and healing I've been going through in my life. The rain for me represents sadness but also healing and growth, as the old is washed away and cleansed with the rain. On that sleepless night last summer, I knew what the title of this book would be.

This book not only talks about my own story of love, loss and healing but it's for anyone that might be going through loss and heartache in their own life. Just know that you will heal through the rain and you too will find your wings and transform into a *Butterfly*

Like you were before.

Cherries

Spring

Oh how lovely the spring time is to me
The trees dance and the flowers again come alive
Clear blue skies and bright shades of green I see
The breeze whistles and nature starts to thrive

To the bloom of plants can nothing compare
Refreshed when this time of year comes around
Wind runs through the grass as it sings with flair
Watching as a light rainfall hits the ground

A time for growth and nourishment is spring
Time to say goodbye to warm winter gear
Color comes back and birds begin to sing
The time to see color restored is here
Oh how lovely the spring is to me
Nature blooming and many sites to see

Written by my daughter
Ashley Chamberlain

Chapters

Grief p. 13

Strength p. 53

Reflection p. 105

Self - Love p. 139

Seasons p. 165

Healing p. 195

Chapter 1

Grief

Feeling it all deeply and saying goodbye to the hurt

She was always a writer
but the moment he broke her
she became a poet

Sometimes when I'm hurting
my mind keeps me awake at night
with stories and poetry
it's during this time
my pen comes alive
when all I want to do is
sleep

I wrote to you
telling you
I miss you
I placed the letter safely in a bottle in the sea
I knew the waves would send you back to me
I watched the water every day for a response
nothing ever came
until one day
your bottle washed back up to me
I could hear the wind say
I sent him back to you
every time you read this letter
you will think of him
and he will always be with you
every day I had you close to me
in the letter
in the wind
and in the

sea

Only the ghosts can sing with me
only the angels can bring me home
so many times I loved
so many songs I needed to sing
so many things I couldn't bring
how many times I needed you home
how many ways we had to go
the stories I couldn't part
I tried to reach your heart
but only the ghosts can sing with me
only the angels can bring me home
so many stories I couldn't sing
so many times the voices rang
heavenly clouds
they brought you home
needed to part
I couldn't breathe
I need you home with me

So many times the angels sing
So many stories you told to me
only the clouds could give you wings
now you're home
so many stories the angels sing
I couldn't reach you next to me
only the ghosts can sing with me
so many ways your presence brings
so many times the clouds covered me
now you surround me

I called through the clouds
To hear your voice
I miss your presence
Here on earth
An eternity of time has passed
But your presence is still needed
How do you say goodbye
To a love you need the most
I miss your warmth
In a world so cold
Your touch alone
Could heal any soul
Your laughter was like sunshine
On the most cloudy day
Your selfless ways always felt like home

They say time heals all pain
You will move on but in a different way

I don't care what they say
I will always need you
I needed you then
I need you now
I need to sink into your arms
I need your warmth

I miss your voice
I miss your laughter
I miss your playful spirit

How does my heart stop aching for you
When I miss you so

I loved you then
I love you now

I know you're here
Through the clouds
Your voice calls out

But sometimes more than anything
I need to feel
you home

I'm always the strong one
always the rock
I pick up the pieces
I fix what's broken
I comfort and listen
I fight for injustice
I protect at all costs
But sometimes
I really wish
For once
I had arms I could fall into
Holding me sobbing
I'm not always strong
I need it too
Someone I trust
To fall into
To pick up the pieces
Of my shattered heart

To fix what's broken
With comfort alone
To let me cry
And scream
No words spoken
Just arms I could fall into
Holding me sobbing
I need it too
The grief is heavy
I carry it daily
While I'm strong
For those around me
But just for a moment
I wish I had arms
I could fall into

I couldnt breathe until I saw your face
So many times
Looking back at me
I needed you then
Like I do now
It wasn't fair
You had to leave
Reaching for you next to me

You had to go
I had to leave
We couldn't stay
I couldn't breathe
Needing you now
You had to leave

You had to go
I had to leave
We couldn't stay
I couldn't breathe
Needing you now
You had to leave

Why can't you stay
Next to me
All of the things
You had to say
To all of the things I had to say
All of the times I had to leave
All of the things we have yet to do
All of the times I missed you

You had to go
I had to leave
We couldn't stay
I couldn't breathe
Needing you now
You had to leave
I had to go
Don't come back for me

I have loved you for 100 years
100 ways I miss you
100 tears fall upon me
100 clouds in the sky above me
100 thoughts in every daydream
100 times I wish it true
100 times I wish you knew
In all the ways, I love you
I'll see you
In 100 *Daydreams*

In the quiet night
The moon shines through
A blanket of white
A sleepless night
The memories kept her awake
Memories of a past
Gentle windswept curtains
Brought the summer breeze
In the quiet of a night
When you were next to me
Talking through the night
I remembered your face tonight
So long ago now
But the memory keeps me awake at night

I couldn't leave your memory rested
When your memory is alive in me
You're too special
To be tucked away
In a chapter in my mind
Your memory stays with me every day
In the sunrise
My morning cup of tea
Listening to the birds
Watching the squirrels
In the comfort of my book
While I make my lunch
In the smell of fresh herbs
Afternoon walks
In the blue slow moving clouds
In the gentle breeze
Watching the trees sway
And the gentle raindrops fall
Your memory is alive
It stays with me

Sometimes she would throw on that old coat of his
She would talk to him as if he was still there with her
She missed him
She would talk about her day
She knew he wasn't there
But his spirit stayed with her

Every day she walked down to that spot on the dock
The place where they once skipped rocks
She couldn't help but think he would be there waiting for her
Every day she held onto her hope
Until one day the wind whispered to her
That he wasn't coming back for her
And that it was time
To let go

You said you loved me
You said you needed me
Just a ghost in a chair
You said don't leave me
You said believe me
I will be there
You left me bleeding
Just a ghost in a chair
You said I'm sorry
You said I'll show you
You said don't go
You said I love you
You made me believe you
Just a ghost in a chair
I was left falling
You left me crying
I needed you there
Just a ghost in a chair
You wouldn't leave me
You wouldn't let me move on from there
You left me angry
You left me thinking
How could I believe
A ghost in a chair

She looks back on a memory with him
They had talked about the future and places they wanted to live
He told her he loved the mountains and that he wanted to live by them
one day
She said, "I'm coming with you, right!?"
He said, "well yeah."
Only things didn't turn out that way
Now here she is looking at the mountains
remembering him

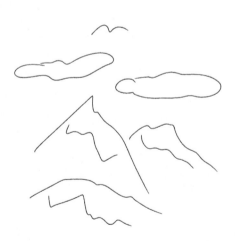

It was the view who found him his lines
And now the poet of love found himself
The view that others are gazing to

How could she be so foolish
Waiting for him
And then he would return
And leave again
Only to show his face again
She would scream at him
Demanding to know what he wanted
It was always him
Unsure of him
Leaving her always breaking
Time and again
How foolish she must have been
But she had enough
And *Forever*

Closed the door
On him

She misses her
She feels so lost without her
Nothing is quite the same
She loves so deeply
And her love was taken away
Her spark is gone
And now she spends her days

Writing away

To distract her from the pain

City bus
City streets
Rainy days
Silk head scarves
And the pattering rain
Falling from
Wet umbrellas
The memories of you
Will never fade

On her wedding day
She didn't forget you
She left you wildflowers down by the water
Where she used to go with you

What a beautiful destiny
Only she isn't yours
The pain you caused her
Awoken the beauty inside of her
Now she is transforming
She is destined for

loving

arms

Every day he walks to the cemetery
He loves to visit her
His longtime love
His only love
He likes to tell her all about his day
And when it's time for him to leave
He watches the trees
And when they blow in the wind
He knows it's her
Telling him
She is listening

He knew she was leaving that day
He drove away
He couldn't watch her leave
It was too sad
She waited in the rain for him
Hoping he would show and tell her not to go
As she stood there
All she could think was
Why am I standing here alone
And she walked away

I saw you last night in my dream
Did I tell you that
I meant to
I guess I was scared of what you would say
But it was nice
It was nice to see you again
Even just for a moment

It's been a long time
And there you were standing right in front of her
You couldn't tell her what you really wanted
She wanted to say
She loves you
She misses you
But again
You just let her
walk away

He will never forget her
There was something in her eyes that he fell in love with
She carried a quiet sadness to her
He wanted to love her
She was beautiful to him
But he couldn't contain his anger
She left him
And now her sadness has turned to light
And every day
He thinks of her

That's the thing about grief
Sometimes it hits you so hard out of nowhere
It's as if the shore is being swallowed by the waves
You hope you don't drown when the water washes over you
You hold on to the shore as you watch the pain wash away
Hoping tomorrow the waves will be calm
As you sleep the pain away
That's the thing about grief
It comes in waves
But the pain eventually disappears with the tide
And tomorrow promises
Gentle

Waves

They both wanted each other
But they couldn't contain their wild
They were ocean's apart
They couldn't contain their wild
So they started to drift away
Wanting each other
But could never contain their wild
So their love drifted away
With the
Ocean's Waves

No one is walking in your footsteps
So how could they possibly know the journey you have endured
The pain your heart has held
The strength it took to overcome
Such heartbreak and still continue walking
No one can judge your story
For you are walking these footprints alone
What they can do
Is walk beside you
Offering a hand to hold
For a journey of pain
Is always better walked
With a hand to hold

Dodging bullets like that old dodge
Screaming echos like those old tires
Falling rain like those old tears
Kissing pain like that old beard
Wasting time like that old chair
Moving on from nothing there

Daytona trip
Two fast track tickets
One last round
27 sleepless nights
The final lap
You drove
I watched the Kansas clouds
The race was over
The rain came down
You drove
I thought it was romantic
As the rain came down
Country fields
But the breeze was cold
I just wanted to go home
But not with you
You never thanked me for the tickets
But at least you got your
Daytona trip
And I got to watch
The Kansas clouds
Alone

I

Dreamt

of flowers by the

Tea

But not the ones you gave

Me

I suppose a sad

Love Story

Makes a great writer

Chapter 2

Strength

You have so much strength, believe in yourself

Even in the darkness
The sun always stays with her

If today you can't find the sun
Remember even the clouds have beauty
And tomorrow watch as the sun
Comes through the clouds

Her entire life people tried to silence her
It's about time she woke up
She has a lot to talk about

No one can take your

Imagination

And your will
To live the life
You dream of

You're a

Beautiful soul

It's as simple as that
Don't let the hate and jealously of others
Diminish who you are

I knew I was leaving
When the walls started closing in
You wanted a wife
But on your terms
Your rules
Your life
I tried to live your way
But my soul was fading
Waiting for you to come home
Dinner on the table
Mindless small talk
But really saying nothing at all
Just a perfect wife
Abiding by the rules
While you live your freedom
Everything is happy
As long as I'm home
I felt like I was crazy
Looking around me
I didn't recognize
What had become of me
Smiling polietly
Doing the laundry
Same suffocating conversations
Oh how was your day

Cherries Chamberlain

I wanted to run away
You never even asked
What I wanted
How I felt
Panic started to come over me
I knew then
I had to free myself
From your cage
I wanted nothing more but to leave
I was determined to break free
I knew it wouldn't be easy
You wanted your way
But you really didn't know me
There is fire in my veins
I didn't want your life
I will always be free
Now all I feel
Is relieved

— in the leaving, she could breathe

I wake up from this beautiful illusion
Thinking I missed you
Not understanding
Why your face is in my dream
A darkened memory
I replaced
But yet I still dream of your face
Does it all have meaning
I only wish to replace your face
And erase your memory
So why does your ghost still haunt me
They say when love runs deep
It's hard to forget
But was it even love I was in
Or the illusion
Of a thought
That love could stand
Maybe a dream
Of what could be
A strong belief
In love covers all
But it's foolish really
For I held on
To a almost what could be
Blinded by the hand
Of a heartless man

Still a romantic daydream
But afterall
Wasn't I in the wrong memory
Holding onto what could be
Of the wrong kind of love for me
Afterall you can't fall in love
With an illusion
A nice ideal
Is a pleasant thought
But after all of that
It simply is just that
An idea of what could be
Wasted on a heartless man
Who doesn't know how to
Daydream
Wiser now
She said goodbye to your memory
A beautiful idea
Tainted by a darkened memory
But love is so much more
Than a beautiful idea
It's everything you are not at your core
And everything she is
Within herself
For you see
True love

Is when you love yourself
To say I'm more
Than your painful memories
For she will always be
A beautiful daydream
And better for leaving him
In his castle of cold darkened illusions

— waking up from a nightmare

Try not to worry about the things going on around you
They quite often work themselves out
Find what gives you peace
And every day you will be calm
No matter what
Is happening around you

Sometimes the light we look for
The light we need
Is closer than we think
We look to the sky
But maybe we should be looking underneath
For the light you need
Was always inside

Don't you know love
You were not made to wait for him
If he were worthy of you
He would never make you wait for him
You are worth so much more
Than someone
That always leaves you waiting

She was always too much for him
She is a force of nature
And he loved her for it
But he doubted his ability to love her
And eventually he blamed her for it
She started to question herself
Wondering if she was too much
He made her feel like there was something
Wrong with her
But she realized
The problem wasn't in her
Like he made her believe all the time
His insecurity and jealousy
Made him a terrible man
For real love doesn't try to shrink you
But will always lift you
And with him
She finally had enough
And never looked back again

— gaslighting and subtle jabs is not love, RUN AWAY

You can spend your entire life dreaming
About where you want to be
It's really a beautiful dream
Or you can find a way to live your dream
If you believe in something with everything you have
You will eventually find yourself
Living out your dream
Where you want to be is waiting for you
Your life begins now

— keep reaching for those dreams until they become your reality

Sometimes to find yourself again
You have to go back to where you started
I can so easily get lost and wrapped up in the world
But left feeling unhappy
Wondering what happened to my life
That's when it's time to go back to where it started
When we were young
It's time to find the things again
That make you feel alive
The things that you love
The things that make you
Who you are
It's time to go back
To the beginning
And start again

— find the things again that truly make you happy

Here we go again
Your plans are coming undone
The big reveal
Under the stars of your circus show
The next act is up
Hope you got your tickets
Because you will like this show
A master of tricks
Under your hat
Of your twisted magic show
But the next act is up
The girl has magic of her own
Is it an illusion
A bad dream of sorts
That your magic is exposed
Your time is up
Your show is old
Refund the tickets
No longer a magician
Just an angry man
To wither away underneath the stars
Of your circus show

Everyone's gone home
The gates have closed
Empty tents of once sold-out tickets
To silent cries of faint goodbyes
Once a magician written in the sky
Now just a man
Left with the memory
Of his circus show

— I refunded my ticket

She is a force just like the sea
Powerful and free
She quietly watches the waves glide in the wind
As the sea begins to rage
In the winds of change
She begins to rise with the sea
For she is a force just like the sea
Powerful and free

She didn't remember asking for your permission
She was born a warrior
Made to fight injustice
She doesn't need your approval
She needs you not to
Stand in her way

You said you loved me
So why did you leave me
I believed that you cared
But you were never there
You played with my mind
But you never cared
When you did, it was taken
Leaving me with my heart breaking
Recklass in your ways
Filling my mind with promises
Knowing my love runs deep
No regard for my heart
Did you think worth keeping
Instead you would flee
With every chance you left me
Only to return again to say you love me
So why were you always leaving
With no regard for whose heart your breaking
Why would you care
When you never have to be there
Always wondering what she wants
But really the one you should have been asking
Is the man that was always taking

The world was waiting for her
All this time
She only needed to go
And when she was done healing
From her pain
That's exactly what she did

— opening up after heartbreak and reaching for your dreams

When they all try to change you
When they all try to tame you
This is when you should transform
Into the

Goddess

That was always in you

Please love
Don't ever listen to anyone that tells you
That you can't be an artist
For you see
It's the artists
That give the world

Beauty

She was there with him
But she didn't feel like he was there with her
All she could think
Was, the door is open
Leave
But she was afraid that if she walked through it
She wouldn't know who she was anymore
But if she didn't leave
She would disappear entirely
So she got her things
And walked through the door

— don't be afraid of new beginnings, especially if where you are isnt safe or good for you

You were made worthy of the best kind of love
Kind love
If someone isn't kind to you
They simply aren't for you

— choose someone that is genuinely kind to you

She knew if she wanted things to change
She would have to muster up every single fiber of courage she had
And make it happen

— he tried to break her but she took her strength back

Maybe she didn't want a relationship
She is too free
Maybe you could see that
But she really loved you
But you couldn't believe that
It didn't take you long to replace her
Maybe she didn't want a relationship
She is too free
Or maybe she could see
She was wasting her time on a man
That didn't really love her
But loved the attention he seeked

She may have left a life of pain behind her
But she intends to spend the rest of her life
Without you
And you will never be welcome
In her story again

She looked in the water
She used to see a reflection of you
But today when she looked in the water
She saw her own reflection

I hope on the days you feel low
That you remember love
You are destined for

Greatness

Everyone told her she couldn't be
An artist
In which she replied, "how do you know
what I can and can't be?"

There will be people who try to take your voice
From you
They will try to suppress you
If you need to
Scream louder

— don't let bullies intimidate you, you are allowed to have a
voice and always reach out for help if you need it

Please remember if they shut the door on you
You never belonged there
Because real love
Never closes the door

There may come a time where you may fall
Completly for the wrong kind of guy
He wears a mask
A well thought out disguise
He will be seemingly kind
And have all of the right things to say
He will comfort you to draw you close
Only to abandon you when you need him most
He will be brave when he needs a hand
But will cower when you reach for his
You will fall and fall hard for him
But when you recognize his disguise
He will no longer have need of you
And you will find yourself fallen
Only this time not into him
Each day will pass
And you will do your best to repair
The shattered pieces
And to learn to stop blaming yourself
For never recognizing
A coward's mask

— please don't blame yourself when someone else is really good at being deceptive

I know you're starting to question things
And wondering if you're on the right path
You can't see where you're going
But remember anyone that ever did anything great
Also faced the unknown, uncertainty, and hardship
Keep fighting forward into the unknown
And watch your path unfold into

Victory

It's exciting to see the road of a champion

— on overcoming opposition and hardship

You weren't made by mistake
You were made to be a champion
You were chosen
Because you fight
You have been knocked down
More times than one can count
But there has been nothing
That can keep you down
You lose a battle
You bleed
You break
And then you rise
Because you're a fighter
They hate you
Because you point out their pride
They break you
Because you break down their mask
They crush you
Because you threaten their plans
You are human
So you fall
You bleed
You break
But you are also

Champion

And then you rise
You are broken
The pain runs deep
You took a few rounds
The wind swept underneath your feet
Your soul crushed
Your body weak
Your beaten down to lie on the cold ground
They mock you
As you try to stand
Your legs give up
Your heart starts to cry
You're foolish if you rise
You're foolish if you try
Her heart sinks
She closes her eyes
She starts to cry
But she can hear a faint
sound
Quietly in the wind
Whisper to her
You are champion
She sinks into the ground
As the wind fades

And then she sees a flash
Of a bright happy face
She can't make out the face
But she hears a little girl's voice
Say, "Momma, I believe in you
I look up to you
I hope I'm a fighter one day just like you."
And she begins to gasp
Her breath returns
The blood rushes through her veins
She can feel the strength rising within
She screams
She picks herself up from the floor
And she screams again in rage
She is back
Only this time
She won't be taken out again
For she is

Champion

— you have incredible strength

Never diminish who you are for anyone else
Embrace your gifts
Embrace your soul
If who you are makes others uncomfortable
Find better people
Who accept the
Beautiful being you are

Your past is heavy
The waters deep
If you focus on it
You will drown
You have fallen into deep water time and again
But you always rose to the surface
Focus on where you want to be and
Swim to that destination
If you trust the water
Instead of fighting it
The water will carry you

You came back for me
But I'm moving on
You broke me
But now you want me
You left me
But now you need me
You loved me
But you hurt me
I stayed with you
But you didn't notice me
Now you can't live without me
You can't just come back to me
When your life is lonely
I loved you
But i've been getting used to
Living without you
You can't just come back for me
Just to leave me
I can't keep going through
This insanity
I don't want to be your daydream
When my heart is bleeding
I'm real
I feel deeply

You left me bleeding
I cried for months
But now I'm standing
I'm moving on
I wanted you
But I stopped
Waiting for you
A long time ago
You can't just come back
Not now
Not like this
Not when I waited for you
I'm sorry
But I need to forget you

— and she permenately walked away

— never wait for someone that ever makes you wait for them

With the love of an uncharted tale
A story unveils
Something simple
Completly profound
Of a broken hearted girl
On a journey all alone
Finds herself in the comfort of a home
Of the strangest place
Where the walls are made of stone
For how could she see
Love within stone
But there inside
Remained even the smallest
Glimmer of hope
For inside the boy
The smallest light
Was her only hope
So she stayed
For in his eyes
She found a home
Even the boy was convinced
He was filled with hope
For he loved the way she felt like home
But you see

When a home is broken
No matter the glimmer of light
It's possible for even stone
To crumble in plain sight
For the boy's light
No longer remained
When the girl started to shine
Brighter in the days
And once where love may have started
With the smallest glimmer
Was now replaced
With hatred and a cage
For the boy simply hated her now
For needing her so
He couldn't bear to let her go
But he couldn't have her stay
And let her light grow
So every day he ripped away
Her only hope
Because he thought
It was the only way
He could get her to stay
In a miserable home
For if he is to remain
Broken and alone

At least she is there
To comfort the days
Where there was once hope
As time went on
The girl remained
Broken and alone
In the cage he made
For you see
It's the comfort of home
Only the love she once saw inside
The promises of home
Was no home she wanted to know
For what comfort can one have
In a home made of stone
Looking into eyes that used to shine
Never understanding
What she could have done
To make him hate her so
When all she ever wanted
Was the comfort of home
Where the girl lives alone
A hope comes along
For within the hate
A new light grows

In the arms of a child
And the comfort of home
For you see this girl on a journey all alone
Really was meant to bring her daughters home
She was no longer alone
For in the arms of hope
A true love shines
And looking back
All she can see
Is now a story
Of how she found her true home
She doesn't remember the pain
For you see
Sometimes a journey
Takes you the wrong way
But does it really?

— she found her way out of the dark and left with her love

She may be small but her strength is
that of the entire ocean

If you focus on the distractions
The disappointment
The heartbreak
That relationship that didn't work out
The people that held you back
The people that hurt you
You will forget who you once were
Before the pain consumed you
All of the distractions were removed
Because they were not making you happy
Why think about unhappy things
When you have a beautiful destination
Right in front of you

Sometimes life will throw you waves of
pain
Every time you come up for air
Another wave takes your breath away
But what if the waves aren't meant to hurt
you
What if the waves are mean't to change
you
What if what feels deeply painful
Is really meant to send you in a different
direction
Resistance will feel like a giant wave
crashing down on you
But instead of resisting the change and
fighting the waves
Maybe it's time to ride the wave
And embrace the change
Maybe it's time to see where this new
direction is taking you

We have always had storms in life in some form
I know it's difficult to deal with
When they're present
But try to remember
Every storm will pass
And don't forget
About the rainbow
That will come
Everything will be calm again

Chapter 3

Reflection

Time to find yourself again

You cannot know yourself in the chaos
You will only know yourself in the silence

I used to believe in love
The fairytale
All that goes with it
The wedding
The cozy home
The happily ever-after

But as the years went by
I found myself falling
Away from this dream

Dreams change they say
Or someone says
Maybe it's just what I say

I can't see that life
Anymore
It's not who I am
It's not what I want
Anymore

The feeling of having
Wings again
Feels like I never lost them
At all
Like they were just waiting for me
To figure it all out
To find myself again

So here we are
A fresh start
A re-do
Back to the beginning
Where it all started
Just a girl
With a different kind
of *Dream*

— finding wings again

I'm drawn to both art and writing
They fit so beautifully together
A poetic love
Of beauty and soul

For every painter a dream takes place
A spark begins inside a heart
To create a world
That the painter believes in
To the world the painter paints
But to the painter
The world is created by the spark ignited
From a heart that dreams
Of a world
That's painted

She holds the world with her pen
Just a simple thing
But quite extraordinary
How she turns her emotions into stories
And all with a simple pen

She loves afternoon walks in the rain
She feels at home
Underneath the rain clouds

Music is her happy place
There is no greater feeling
Than to pick up an instrument
And to feel the music
Run through her

She's A

Lovely girl

With a

Very old soul

She is

Wildfire

And fields
Of honey

She loves to watch the birds in the trees
Listening to their melodies
She often wonders
What exactly
They are saying

She loves the smallest moments in life
Like simply standing in the rain
With you laughing
As the rain kisses her skin

She wasn't made for glass slippers
She was made to feel
The earth beneath her feet

Hair of golden wind
Skin as cool as morning day
Lovely
Wild
Beautiful
And
Free

For living as a stone puts the ocean to death
She can't survive in the cold embrace
For she needs an ocean of depth

Her spirit connects with nature
She understands the winds
She understands the storms
She understands the animals
She understands the trees
She understands the rain
She was born with

The spirit of the earth

She has this way of taking

B

R

O

K

E

N

Things and making them

Beautiful

She wants to live a quiet life
But she gets this feeling
She was made for more

Sometimes when the chaos around her is too much
She goes to the river
She loves the feel of the water
It's the one place
She feels at peace

You're a bird
You were given wings to

Fly

All you have to do is use them

When she was young
She would climb trees and watch the clouds go by
She loved how beautiful and peaceful
They looked floating in the sky
She often wondered how no one else
Ever seemed to notice them
But it didn't matter
This was her place
In her tree
Where she would go to get away
Even if just for a little while
To take in all the beauty she could see

Take time for yourself
Everyone needs a break
Time to just be
Find a place that makes you happy
And just sit there for awhile
The soul needs to rest
And to be surrounded by nature
Take time today
Just for you

— it's ok to take a break when you need to

It might be hard for a little while
You're going to miss him
He was a part of your story
But if you shut yourself off to every other possibility
You just never know
Life could be handing you the
greatest part of your story
Let love in again
Miss him
Think of him
And remember to live again

She is golden like the sun
She is calm like the breeze
She is grounded like the earth
She is healing like the sea

Connect yourself to the earth
Walk barefoot in rain puddles
Climb trees
Pick lilacs right after it down pours

She can feel the rhythm of the waves
The waters are calm
But she can feel the energy underneath
The energy is being shifted her way
The waves are rising
Something incredible is headed her way
No one understands it
But she feels it

— if you believe in your dream, you don't need anyone else to believe

Cherries Chamberlain

She loves rainy days
There is nothing like the cool feel
Of the water on her skin
With her camera in hand
She loves to capture the beauty of the
Fresh water on the trees

— beauty is all around us

Connection lives within nature
The trees are connected to the earth
The animals are connected to the trees
The water is connected to the soil
Nature longs for your connection
When you connect yourself to the earth
Your spirit is still
You become one with nature
And everything is calm

Find a beautiful place
Stay there for awhile
And take in all you see
It's in this moment
You'll find life
Life isn't just in the non-stop day to day
Life is in
All the little things
That make time stand still

Remember her
There she is
That girl
That can see beauty
Through a lens

— find the things again that make you happy

She spends every day
Taking in every moment
And every moment
She takes in
Is beautiful

Chapter 4

Self - Love

You deserve to be loved too

She doesnt care what people think of her
She cares about love
She cares about fairness
She cares about equality
and kindness
She cares about growth
She cares about people
But she doesn't care
What people think of her
She is her own person

— a person's true nature is felt, people aren't perfect but a good person
will acknowledge their faults, will grow and love people

Don't be afraid to walk
alone sometimes
You just may be walking
towards
Everything you want

— some days can feel lonely but it's just temporary, take this time to
do something that makes you happy - work on that project you
always wanted to do - spend time getting to know yourself - you
won't always feel lonely

You can't let go of the past
Because you loved him
But now you spend all of your days
Without him
Expressing all of your grief, frustration and anger
Through your tears
The only way you know how to remain sane from the madness
You came out of
That's the thing about love
We feel it
We need it
We think about it
It moves us
It blinds us
Its the force that drives us
And sometimes it can come for a reason
And for a season
Sometimes it may not even be what you really wanted
But I have found that through the madness, the anger and the sadness
You see yourself more clearly
And when looking back you realize
You couldn't see yourself at all
And you're grateful to have come out of the madness
The real love in all of it
Was looking back at you in the mirror through all the sadness
He wasn't who you needed to love
It was the girl that thought she needed his love
And now when you look in the mirror
There is a reflection of *Love*

Keep on dreaming love
For dreams are what
You're made of
And if you ever
Lose your way
Remember
You will always
Be made of
Dreams

I've tried love
I've tried big love
I've tried figuring it out
I've tried staying
I've tried understanding
I've tried living in the moment
I tried to see you
I tried to be with you
It felt like big love
But why couldn't I see me
I loved you
Your smile
Your laugh
Your quirky ways
But I didn't see me with you
I didn't see me at all
I had to leave
Because I needed to love me
You've moved on
With someone new
And that's ok
Because through it all
I realized what I
Really needed
After all this time
Was to be free
Of it all

You are worthy of love
Do not let your past or your mistakes
Decide the amount of love you
Should have
Do not let the harsh judgements of others
Decide who you are
Because the thing is
There is not a single person
Without a mistake
Who hasn't fallen
Who hasn't cried
Who hasn't asked for forgiveness
You may not be perfect
No one is
But one thing will always
Remain true
Your heart is good
And no matter
What happens
You are always

Worthy

Of love

They wanted to write your story for you
But you're much too independent
For that nonsense
You have always known
You write your own story
Do not let someone else
Be the narrator for your life
After all
It is
Your life

Her favorite kind of Sunday
Will always be
Pajamas
Cozy blankets
Warm tea
And a book
She just can't put down

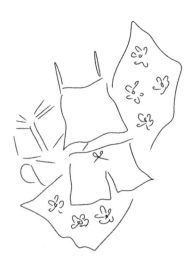

People say they want things that are
Relevant and current
She could care less how relevant and current
Something is
She cares about the heart
Of things
She will never stand for anything
She doesn't believe in
She believes in one thing
Love
If something doesn't speak love
She doesn't want to be a part of it
She will not conform
Blame it on her
Rebellious nature

Dear future self,

Try not to be so hard on yourself - life is hard for everyone

It's ok you loved the wrong guy - you loved him in the moment - he wasn't good for you - but it doesn't mean it wasn't important - it was how you felt

Don't listen to anyone's advice (unless you trust them) on what your path is or should be - they have a different path - so how are they able to know what yours is

Doesn't matter how old you are - if you like that hairstyle or you like that dress or you like that book - if something makes you happy but it's childlike - let it make you happy

Try not to be so sad when things end - if the magic is over - simply create it - after all you're magical

But most importantly - remember that every part of your journey is a little piece of who you are - the good and the bad - will always show you the way to what your heart actually desires

Trust yourself - you know yourself
best

And always love yourself - there is
only one of you in the entire world
and the world needs you

Now go and create something
beautiful for others or simply just
for yourself

And live your life free of the
opinions of others

Love,
Your heart

— a love letter to you

The louder the voices became
The more the doubt sank in
All she ever heard
Was that she needed to be
Someone else
To do something else
But she thought
How can i possibly be
Someone other than me
If i can't seem to fit in
There must be something
Wrong with me
Why do I daydream
When others live in reality
Why do I see beauty in the broken
When others see the broken
Why do I see shades of green in the leaves
When some see just a leaf
Why does the rain make everything shine
When to some
The rain is wet and cold
There must be something
Wrong with me
Or maybe
Just maybe
There is nothing wrong with me

But that
It's the artist in me
I was made to be me
To paint the colors of the sea
To capture a moment in time
With a camera in hand
To write all the stories
To sleep under the stars while
The fireflies dance above me
In a world lost at sea
What would I be
If I couldn't be an artist
It doesn't matter to me
Because I would never want to be
Anything but me
It's the artist in me

— it's the artist in her

She is an artist
Criticized all her life for this
But she loves this
About herself

Remember when you were young
And you played and ran through
Fields and puddles
Let's bring this girl back
She is still inside of you
It's time for you
To be

Happy

She loves the simple things life has to offer
Like ocean waves
Raindrops
And
Love notes

Take a little time
Find a little space
And create something beautiful
Not for anyone else
But just for you
So every day
You have something beautiful
To look forward to

When she was young
She would build beautiful forts
Made from sheets, sticks, and nails
Filled with blankets, pillows, lights and books
No one understood her
She often felt alone
But this was her place
The one place she felt safe
And not alone
For she had her stories
Stories of adventures, love, and of people just like her
That also felt alone
She didn't know where her place was in the world
But there in her place of sheets and books
She was never alone
Because she always had someone to go on
Adventures with in her stories
Safely tucked away
In her own little world
Wrapped up in her
Blankets and books

I know that first chapter really hurt you
I know you are disappointed with how it turned out
You wanted so badly for it to work out
You put your entire heart into it
But the reason you aren't in that place anymore
Is because they didn't put their entire heart into you
You were taken out because you deserve better
You deserve the amount of heart you put in
Now is the time to fall in love again
To fall in love with your life
To fall in love with photography again
To fall in love with designing again
To fall in love with exploring and traveling
To fall in love with books again and writing stories
Now is the time to fall in love again
With that girl that was left behind
But still has all those beautiful things
that make her shine

Fall in love again

For all the dawn I wish through the fog
Of a life I loved
With not a single pain
The tears I've cried
My life away
Choices made
Crumbled away
I lift my eyes
Beyond the clouds
Wishes come down
Like rain
Tears are made
But pain washes
Away
To a life I love
A life meant for me
The tears are gone
The rain has stayed
But now I'm covered
In raindrops of love

— healing

Always the romantic
Never any good at romance
But she always thought
That one day
She might
Figure it out

You thought he was the sun
You thought he was the waves
You thought he was the rain
You thought he was everything

Don't you realize
You are the sun
You are the waves
You are the rain
You never needed him

You are everything

Chapter 5

Seasons

A time for change and new beginnings

Don't worry about summer ending
Fall will soon begin and the once noisy streets
Will be filled with falling leaves
Quietly blowing through the air
The days will be filled with comfort
Warm cozy sweaters
Apple picking and dancing in leaves
Magical days are on the way
You will see a change when the colors fade
New beginnings are in the air

— to new *Beginnings*

She is comforting like the autumn wind
She has this way about her
That will always feel like

Home

There's this thing about fall
When everything seems to come back to you
Those memories of a grandmother's laughter
Those memories of a long ago love
And yes, the memories will always stay with you
But sometimes fall
Can bring new beginnings
A time for change
Although you don't want to let go
And you never have to
of all those beautiful memories
But instead of fearing the unknown
Maybe this fall
Will bring
New happy memories
Maybe this fall
Will bring new love
A love that feels like home

The wind

Dances

With the leaves

She

Dances

With the rhythm of the trees

She loves the peace the Autumn brings
With the warm colors of the Autumn leaves
And the aroma filled air
Of pumpkin and spice
There is this gentle breeze
That the cool Autumn wind brings in
It's in Autumn
She feels at peace

Sometimes on a rainy Sunday morning
You just want some warm cocoa
and a little

Extra

Chocolate too

There is nothing more comforting to her
Than her cozy sweater
And

Teacup

In the morning rain

Lazy mornings
Cozy socks
And a little bit of

Honey

Too

Right in the middle of her
sorrow and tears
Love washes in
In the cold
Autumn rain

All she wanted to do on the
Rainy fall day
Was get lost in her book

Just another cozy autumn morning
Listening to the rain
She closes her eyes
And

Dreams

The words come off the page
They float through the air
Like the fresh autumn breeze
Dew drops of rain cover her skin
It's a comforting feeling
As the autumn leaves
Whisper
I love you
She was finally free

— healing after a painful relationship and finding your
voice again

It's in the quiet of the January breeze
That her love touches you gently
She whispers through
The

Winter

Wind
Softly
I love you

No one wants to play
Everyone around me is so serious
I miss the laughter
I miss the fun
I miss the carefree easy days
Now I'm all alone
Just wanting to play
But everyone around me seems to age at a faster pace
It's only serious days

All i want to do is build a fort in the snow lying in
the cold
Watching the snowflakes fall from the stars

But I'm left lying all alone
Because I'm the only one around me that sees the
magic in the stars

Everyone else has gone away
Or maybe I just imagined them there

Under the fallen snowflakes

The cold brings me back to life

Sometimes I can't stand being an adult
Never laughing
Never playing
Never lying in the cold
Watching snowflakes fall from stars

Maybe one day someone will understand

But for now I'll lie here watching

While the cold
Falls from the stars

—romanticizing life

Meet her in the

Meadows

Where the birds sing
Underneath the

Fallen snow

Winter dreaming
Flowers
Paper and Pen
And a heart
Full of stories

The whispers of the trees
Pale blue sky
A long journey behind
Windswept breezes
A new season
Changes
To a path once unseen
The wind tells her a
New story
Just beneath the blowing of
The trees
Was always a path
She just needed to
Believe

Did you want a little reminder of spring
buy yourself some flowers
They really are
Always lovely

Beautiful white sunflowers
The past is behind you
Look for the flowers
You always have a new beginning

She felt spring in the air
As the cool morning breeze
Swept her skin and
Raindrops
Fell from the clouds

Spring is in the air
She missed her time by the river
Where time stands still
As she watches the river flow
She loves the water under her feet
And the gentle wind on her skin
Listening to the birds sing

Waiting for April
A sign of spring
A rainy day
A blue bird or two
Puddles and puddles
Maybe umbrellas too
But one thing is for sure
Count on a flower or two
When spring blooms
Open the windows
Listen to the rain
Feel the breeze
The smell of the earth
After the rain
And the blue birds sing
You can always count on spring

Just your typical Saturday
Coffee
Reading
Croissants

and
daydreaming
of a
beautiful love
story

She loves her Sunday afternoons
of farmers markets and

Flowers

Like the changes in the wind
Spring may just bring you love again

Chapter 6

Healing

Through all the healing
She found her

Wings

She is a butterfly

— fly freely

She has been asleep for so long
Living in her world of hurt
But something is starting to awaken inside of her
She is healing and her wings
Are being restored
She is transforming
And becoming a

Butterfly

Like she was before

To all the stories never told
Asleep for so long
She is finally awake
To tell the stories

Connect yourself to nature
It has the ability to heal and restore
Watch the subtleties of the earth
The answers are there
Let go and listen

— spend some time in nature and you will feel peace

The wind is calling you

Love

Home
To wild fields

The water is healing for her soul
And every time she is near it
It calms her instantly
It washes away her pain

Take some time away darlin
Come play some music by the water
nothing heals the soul
Like music and water

There is an entire world of

Breathtaking

Moments
waiting for you
All you have to do
Is go

The painter paints of the beauty of the surface
But the writer writes of the
Beauty of the

Soul

She has this loving kind of way
She can be fierce when needed
But she also has a
Healing gentle way

If you wake up every day believing that
Something beautiful is about to happen
Then every day
Something beautiful
Will happen

She needs things with soul
Deep rooted trees
The songs the birds sing
The flow of the river
The grounding of the earth
The air we breathe
The depth of the ocean
The stillness of the mountains
Her soul needs to be
Connected to things with soul

It's so calming when you look
Up at the clouds
Wrap yourself in the blanket of blue
Get lost in the white airy stillness
Let your worries fade away
For a moment
Let yourself be present
In the stillness

— take your mind off your worries, look up at the clouds and breathe

She is a simple serenity
She is healing
She has a lightness to her now
She has peace

When the rain falls
Remember that's when
Everything grows
Don't worry about the rain
It's only meant to heal you

When the days seem long
And the nights uncertain
Hold onto your hope
Close your eyes
And remember the dawn brings
New light
This too love
Is temporary

Nature will always heal a broken spirit
If you need healing
Find your way back to nature
And watch as it restores your
Heart

She loves to just sit quietly watching the view
The water will always be calming to her
Life was made for simple
Mornings like this

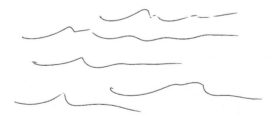

You feel lost in the desert
Keep walking
Just on the other side
Is an

Ocean

Of healing

I know the first couple chapters were difficult
But turn the page
The next chapter is filled with unexpected surprises
And a world of happiness
For you
Because you deserve it

Don't worry if you can't find any flowers
Keep walking until you do

All things grow in their own time
Don't worry love
If you can't seem to get
To where you want to be
With a little patience
And a little time
Just like a flower blooms
you too
Will grow

To mend her heart
She is going to plant
Lots and lots
Of flowers

....but instead - it started Raining Flowers

We've made it through
All the heartache
The loss, the tears
We've made it here
To this moment
Will we always remember that pain
Maybe
But does it have to be
Our future
No, it doesn't
We are healing
We will be happy
We will love life again
We will fly
With

Butterfly Wings

— with love

About The Author

Cherries Chamberlain is a writer and artist. She has been writing, drawing, and designing from a very young age. She has always had a love for creativity and telling stories. She went through some difficult times growing up, writing helped her get through these hard times. Throughout her life, her voice was taken away from her, but over time she found her strength and her voice and now she writes words of love, loss and healing that she shares with the world through her poetry, quotes and stories.

She loves the ocean, rainy days, writing poetry, writing and illustrating children's books, watching the stars, waterfalls, getting lost in nature or getting lost in a bookstore. She has future plans to write fantasy novels, romance novels, children's books and more poetry.

Her next poetry books
Raining Flowers
Raindrops and Clouds

You can find her on Instagram
@ cherriesnoelchamberlain

Thank You

To all of you that have continued to support my writing. Through Instagram I've been able to meet and connect with the sweetest people around the world that always send me kind messages of love and encouragement. I appreciate all of you so much! You have all helped me heal and now I hope this book helps you heal, gives you some hope or makes you smile. I'm so thankful to have all of you!

To my daughters

Thank you for always believing in me and encouraging me to pursue my dreams. I will always encourage you to follow your dreams. I'm excited to see all of the beautiful things yet to come for both of you! I'm so incredibly thankful God placed two sweet girls in my life, I love you!

To my mom

Thank you for encouraging me to keep going when some days I wasn't sure if I had it in me to do this because of the hurt I was trying to heal from. Right when I needed it most, you gave me the words I needed to keep going. I'm incredibly grateful for your love and encouragement, I love you!

To my grandma Sally and my sisters

Although grandma you aren't here, your spirit always stays with us. I can feel you all around us and your words have always stayed with me. You told me I could be anything I wanted to be and not to let anyone tell me otherwise. You were always a dreamer and you let me believe in dreams, I will always be grateful for this! You introduced me to my love of books and aunt Jenny introduced me to my love of art. With the influence of both of you I discovered a world I would forever love of reading and creativity, thank you to you both, I love you! And to my sisters, thank you for helping me find my way at times I felt lost and didn't know what to do with my life. You reminded me of my love for story telling and art, you helped me get back on the path I was always meant to be on, thank you for this, I love you!

Made in the USA
Monee, IL
30 September 2024

66302296R00125